Ages 3+

Disney LEARNING

XAR

Sm

Numbers & Counting

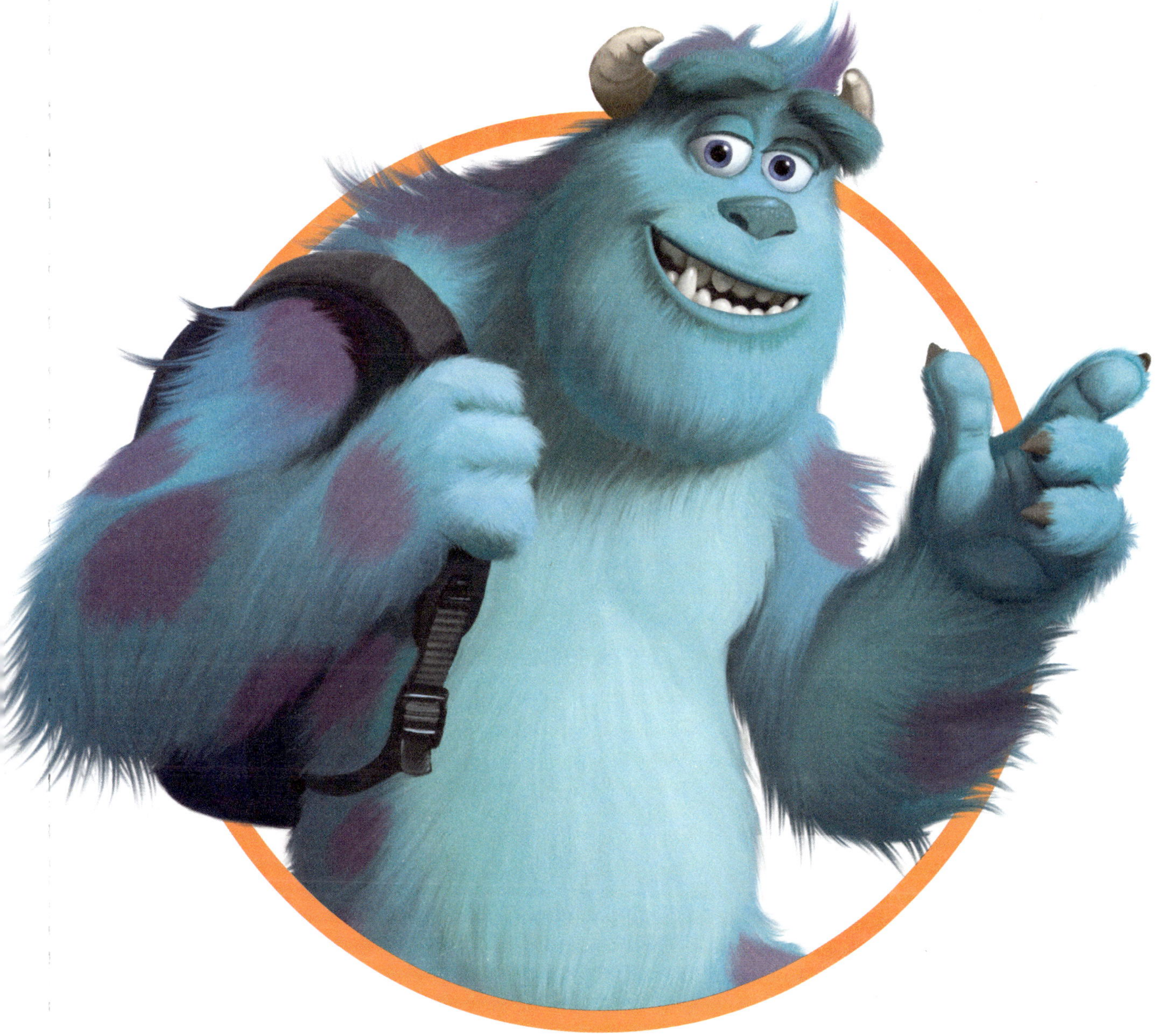

Carson Dellosa Education
Greensboro, North Carolina

Published by
Carson Dellosa Education
PO Box 35665
Greensboro, NC 27425 USA

ISBN 978-1-4838-6146-3
01-053217784

Contents

0

There is nothing on the plate.
All the food is gone.
If there is no food, you can say there is **zero** food.
Trace and print the number **0**.

Learn Together

Use empty containers to help your child understand the concept of zero. Example: "We had one egg left in the carton. We used it to make muffins. Now we have no eggs left. We have zero eggs!"

0 or **zero** means nothing. Circle the objects that have nothing inside.

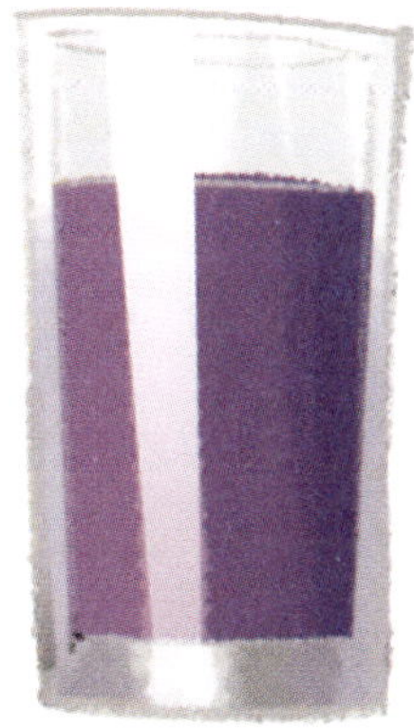

1

Mike has 1 eye.
Trace the number 1.
Print the number 1.

1

Circle the monster with 1 eye.

2

Bing-Bong has 2 bags.

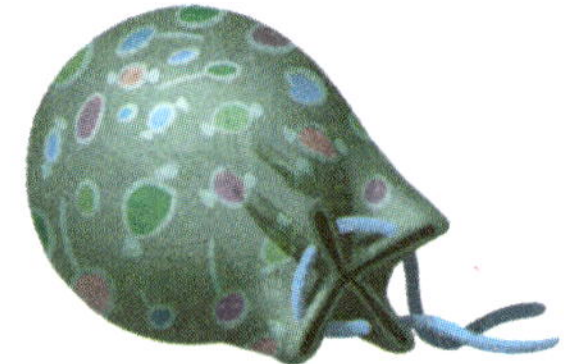

Trace the number 2.
Print the number 2.

2 2 2 2 2 2 2

Joy and Sadness are collecting memory orbs. Circle the group that has **2** memory orbs.

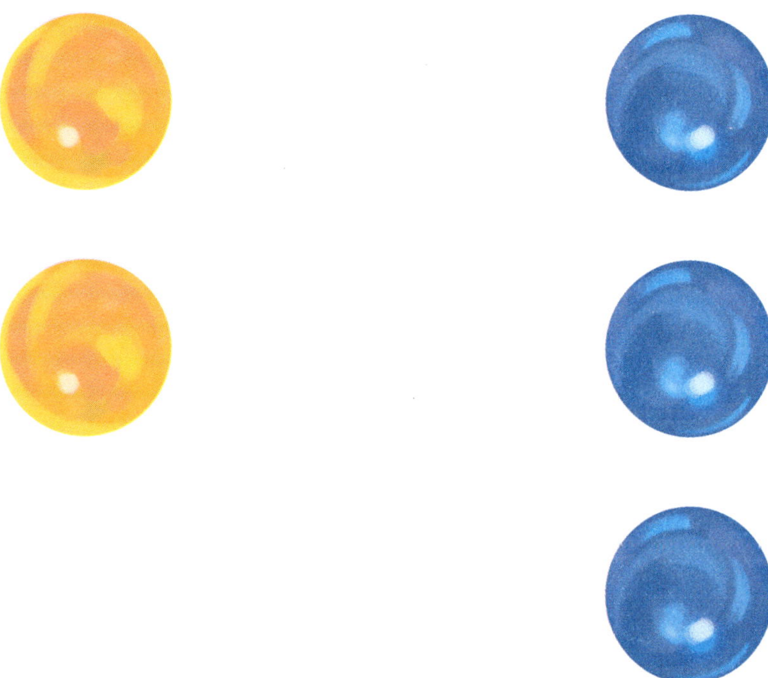

3

Art has 3 skateboards.

Trace the number 3.
Print the number 3.

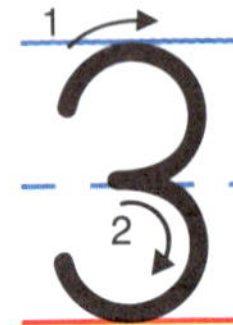

3 3 3 3 3 3 3

This monster has **2** heads!
Draw a monster with **3** heads.

Elastigirl sees 4 motorcycles.

Trace the number 4. Print the number 4.

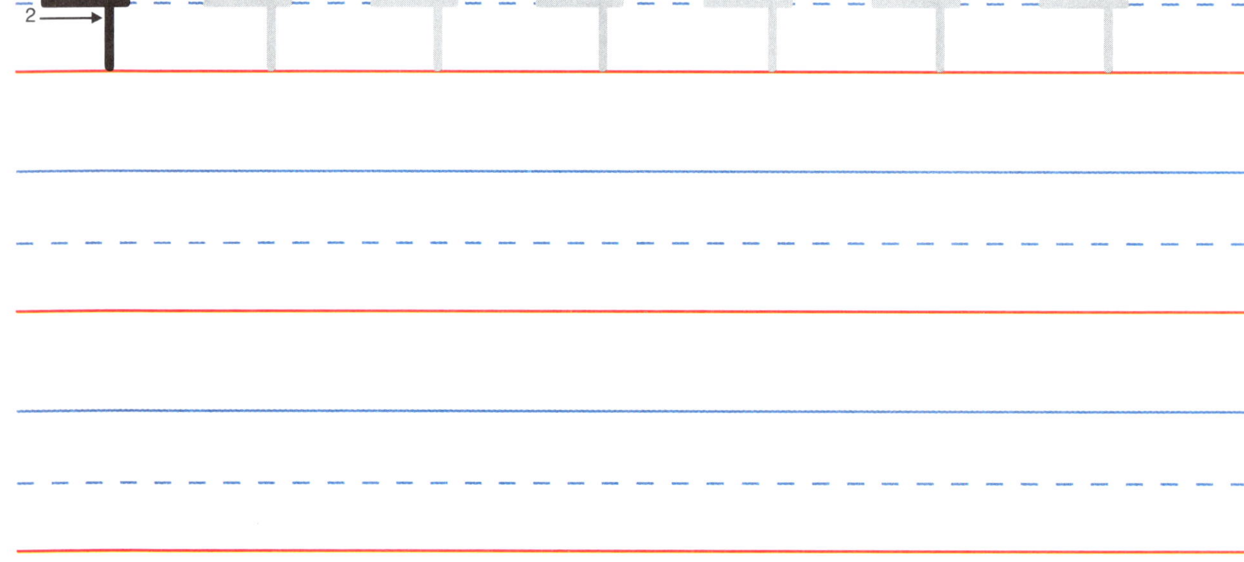

Circle **4** bottles for Jack-Jack.

5

Joy juggles **5** memory orbs.
Trace the number **5**.
Print the number **5**.

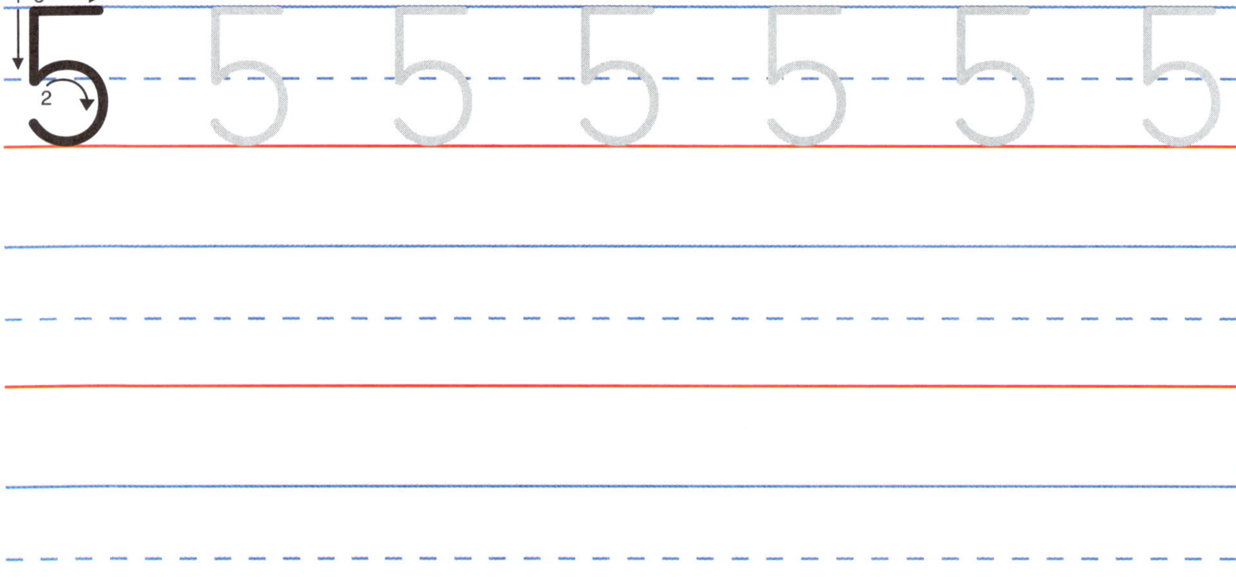

Connect the dots from **0** to **5**. Then, color.

Winston has 6 vehicles.

Trace the number 6.
Print the number 6.

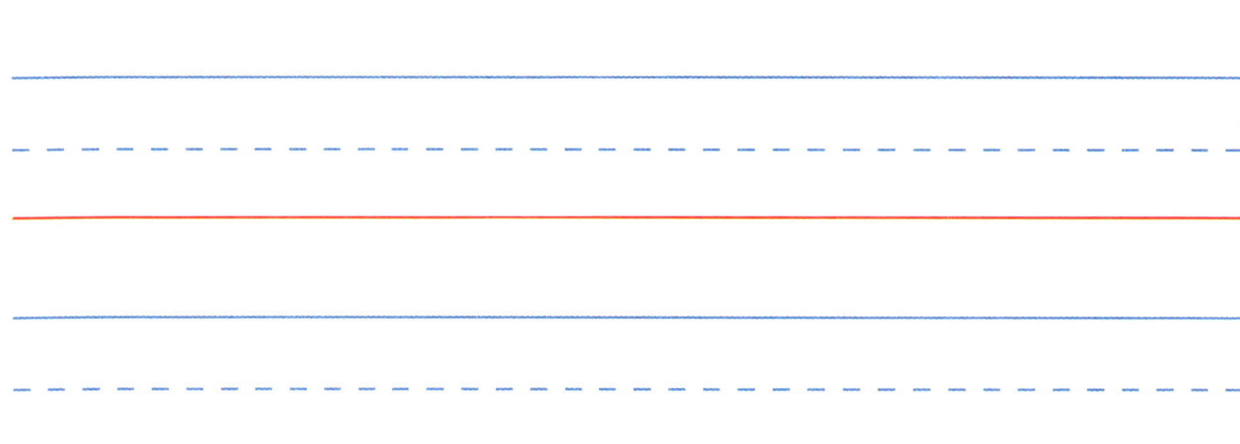

Help Elastigirl find Screenslaver!
Connect the path from **1** to **6**.

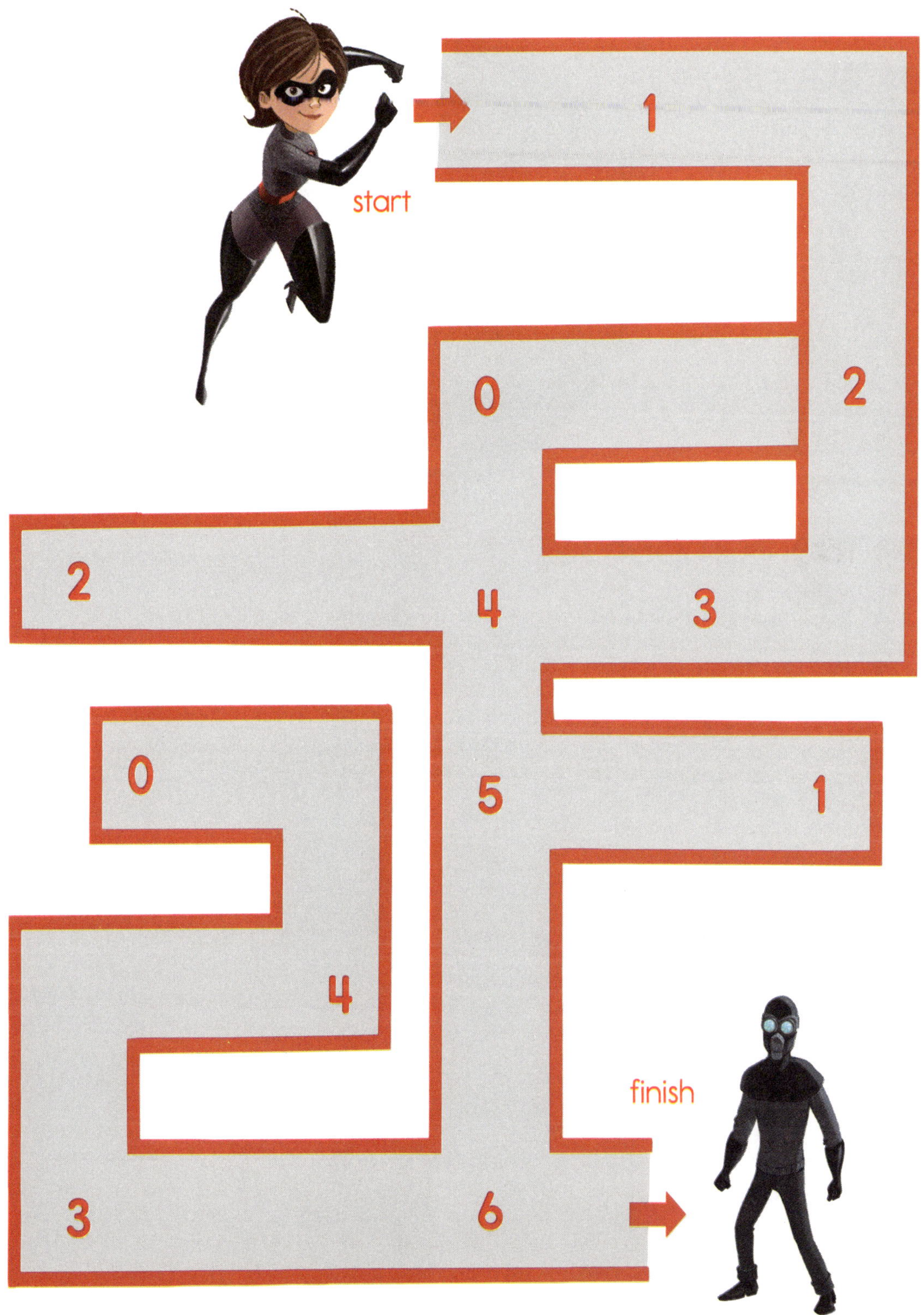

7

Sulley counts 7 soccer balls.

Trace the number 7.
Print the number 7.

7 7 7 7 7 7 7

Draw more balls to make 7 in all.

8

Bing-Bong counts 8 sheep.

Trace the number 8.
Print the number 8.

Connect the numerals to the number words.

9

Squishy counts 9 bikes.

Trace the number 9.
Print the number 9.

9 9 9 9 9 9 9

Connect the dots from 1 to 9. Then, color.

10

Jack-Jack sees **10** raccoons.

Trace the number **10**.
Print the number **10**.

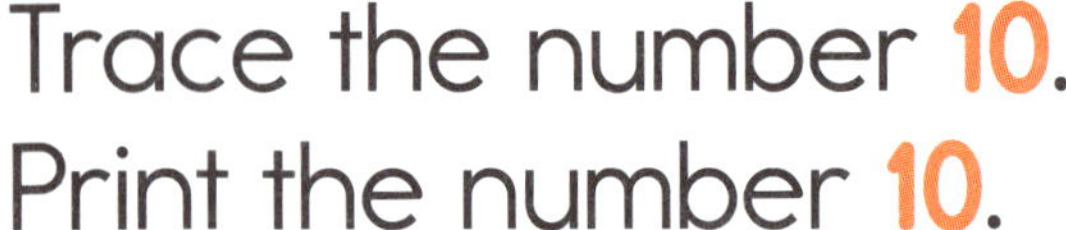

Dash wants **10** strawberries for a snack.
Draw **10** strawberries on the plate.

Learn Together

Help your child trace both hands on a piece of paper. Your child can write a number above each finger and thumb, starting with 1 on the left and ending with 10 on the right.

Count the items in Bob's office. Write the number.

=

=

=

=

Count the pens.

=

Count the books.

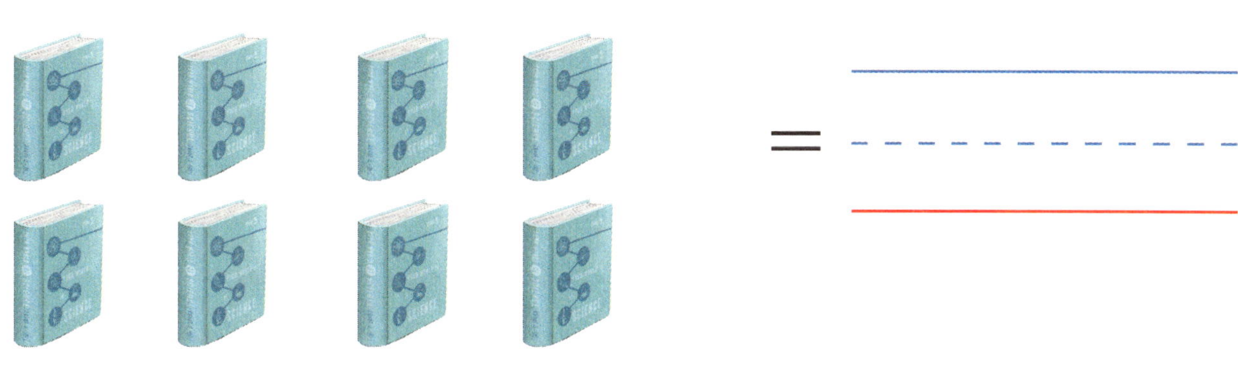

=

Count the trash cans.

=

Smart Skill: Numbers 0–10 Review

Mike is collecting things for school.
Match each number to the correct group. The first one is done for you.

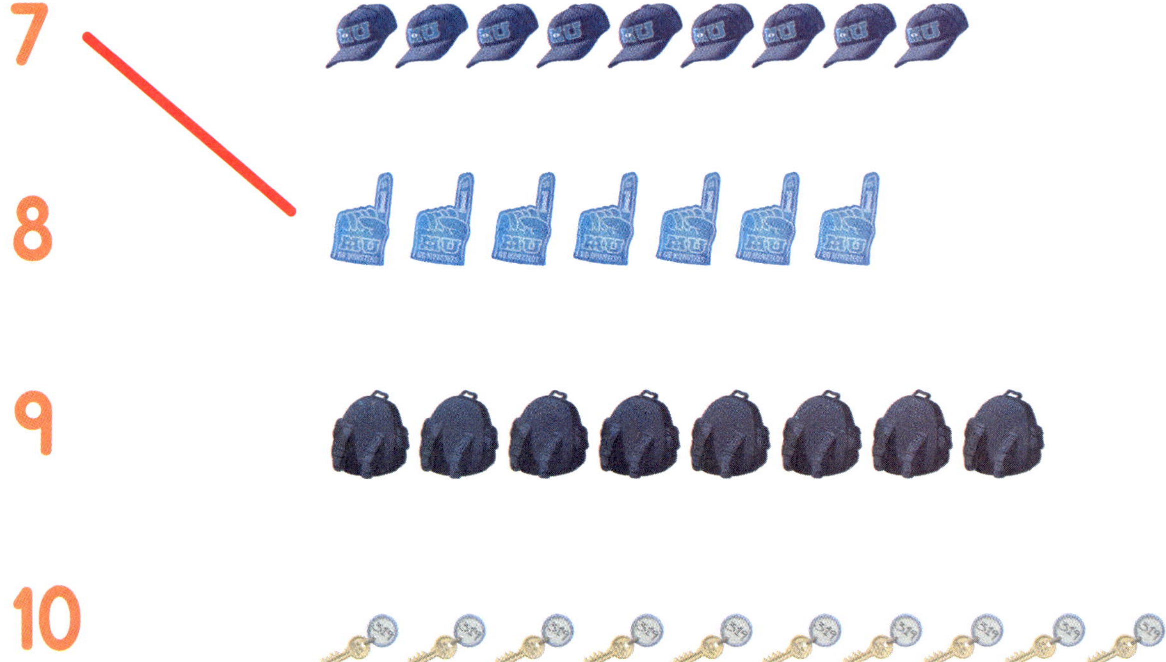

How many books does Mike need? Match each number to the correct number of books. The first one is done for you.

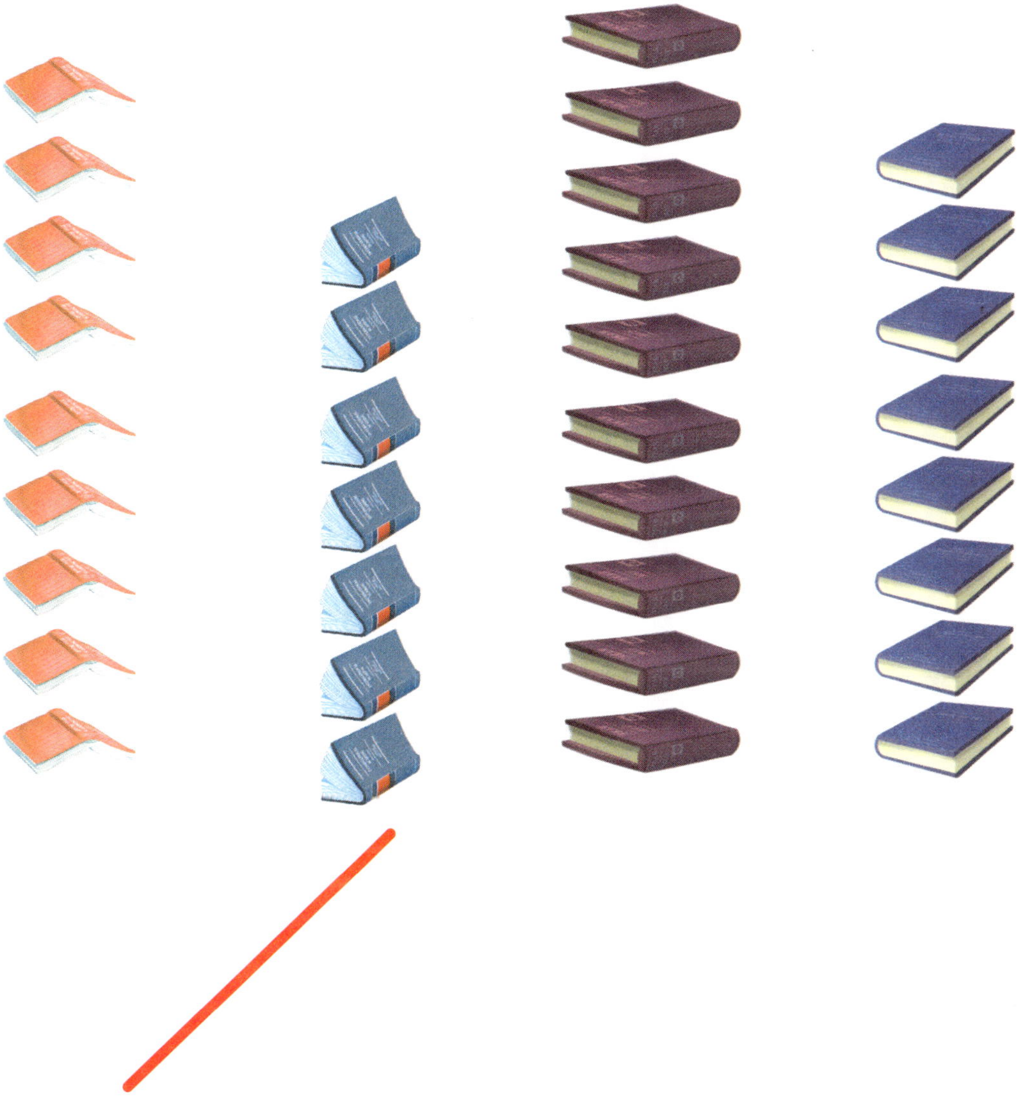

7 8 9 10

11

Joy counts 11 puzzle pieces.

Trace the number 11.
Print the number 11.

1 1

Find the hidden 11s.

12

Sulley gets **12** drinks for his friends.

Trace the number **12**.
Print the number **12**.

12 12 12 12 12

Mike needs **12** books for his classes. Draw more books to make **12**.

13

Dash is doing homework.
He has **13** pencils.

Trace the number **13**.
Print the number **13**.

Dash's locker is number 13. Circle it.

14

Mike has 14 suitcases.

Trace the number 14.
Print the number 14.

Circle 14 balloons.

15

Edna is getting **15** boxes delivered.

Trace the number **15**.
Print the number **15**.

Bob has **15** mugs.
Circle the group with **15**.

Learn Together

Gather a group of 15 small items (buttons, crayons, blocks). Give your child 10 items and keep 5. Ask your child, "Who has more?" Take turns.

16

Riley hits **16** pucks.

Trace the number **16**.
Print the number **16**.

Draw **16** memory orbs.

17

Mike has 17 hats.

Trace the number 17.
Print the number 17.

Draw a pizza with **17** toppings for Sulley.

18

Lucius counts **18** phones.

Trace the number **18**.
Print the number **18**.

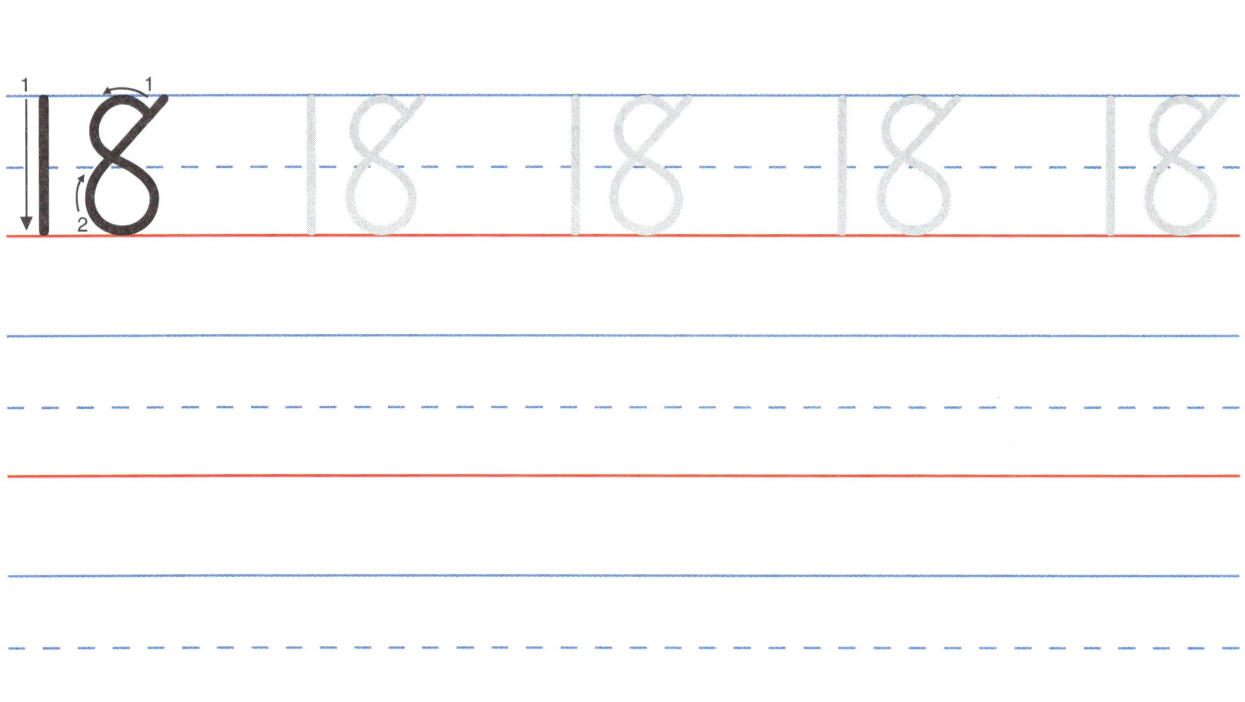

Count each group of objects.
Draw more to make **18**.

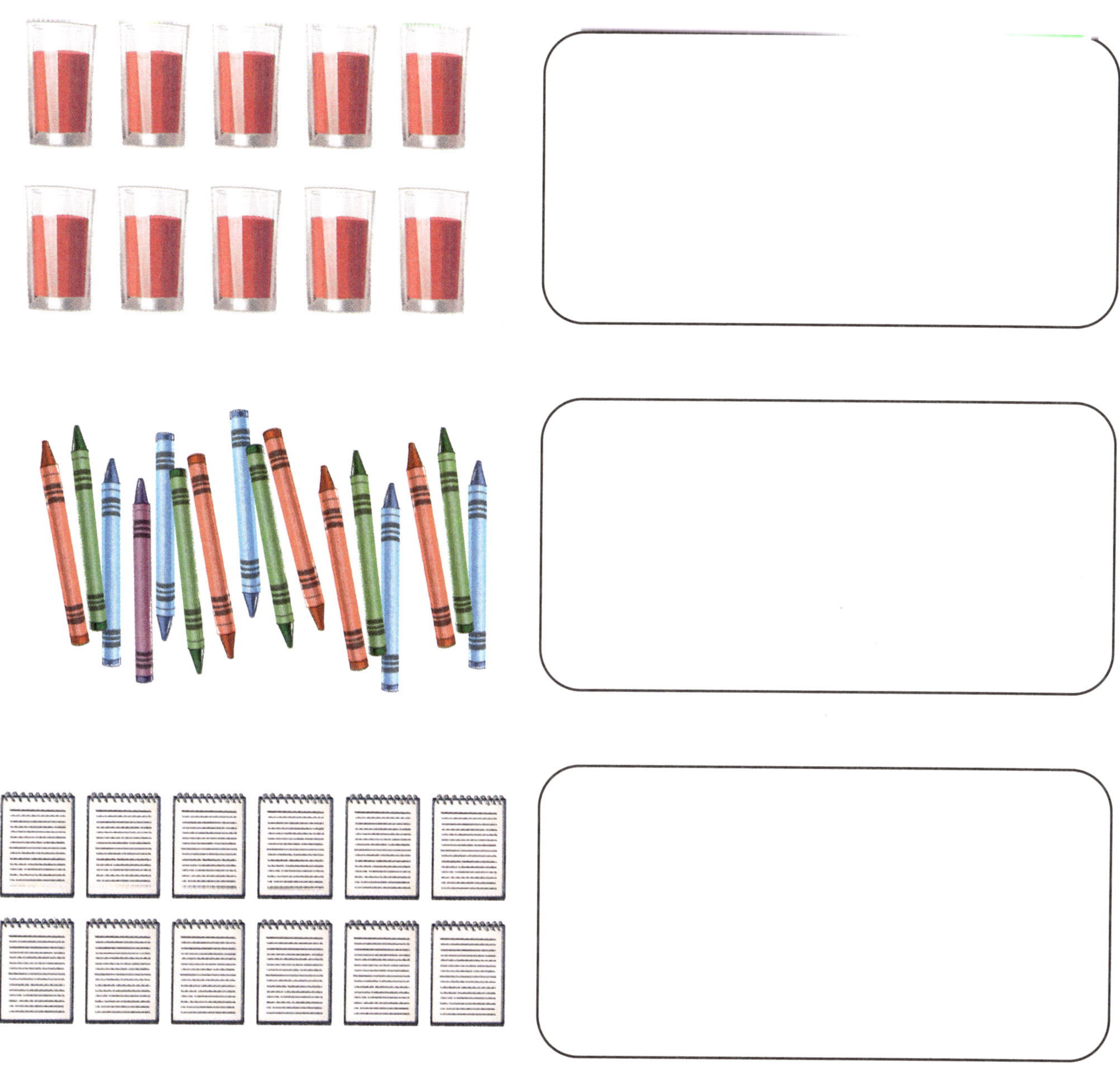

Learn Together

With your child, gather similar objects (pencils, crayons, blocks). Ask your child to make a pile that has 18 objects.

19

Dean Hardscrabble has 19 scream canisters.

Trace the number 19.
Print the number 19.

Find the hidden 19s.

20

Bing-Bong has 20 candies.

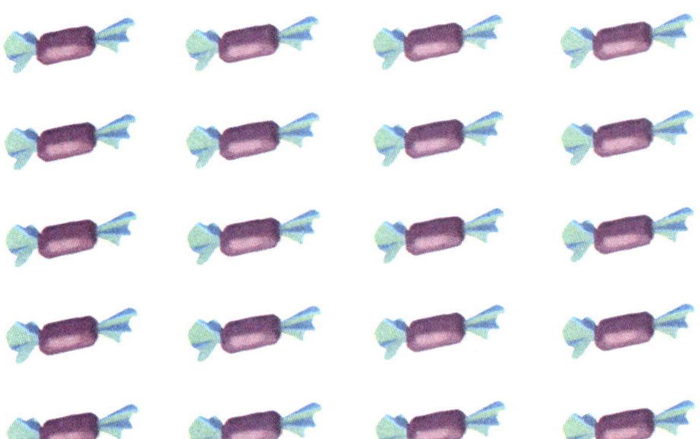

Trace the number 20.
Print the number 20.

Find the hidden numbers 15 to 20.

Joy can count to **20**.
Can you?

0 1 2 3 4 5
6 7 8 9 10
11 12 13 14 15
16 17 18 19 20

Print the missing numbers.

___ 1 ___ 3 4

5 6 ___ 8 9 10

11 ___ ___ 14 15

___ 17 ___ 19 20

0 ___ 2 3 4

15 ___ ___ 18 19

13 14 ___ 16 17

Learn Together

With your child, count objects around your home. Example: "How many books are on the shelf?" Encourage them to point to the objects and count out loud.

Connect the dots from 1 to 20. Then, color.

Help Bob find Jack-Jack. Connect the path from 1 to 20.

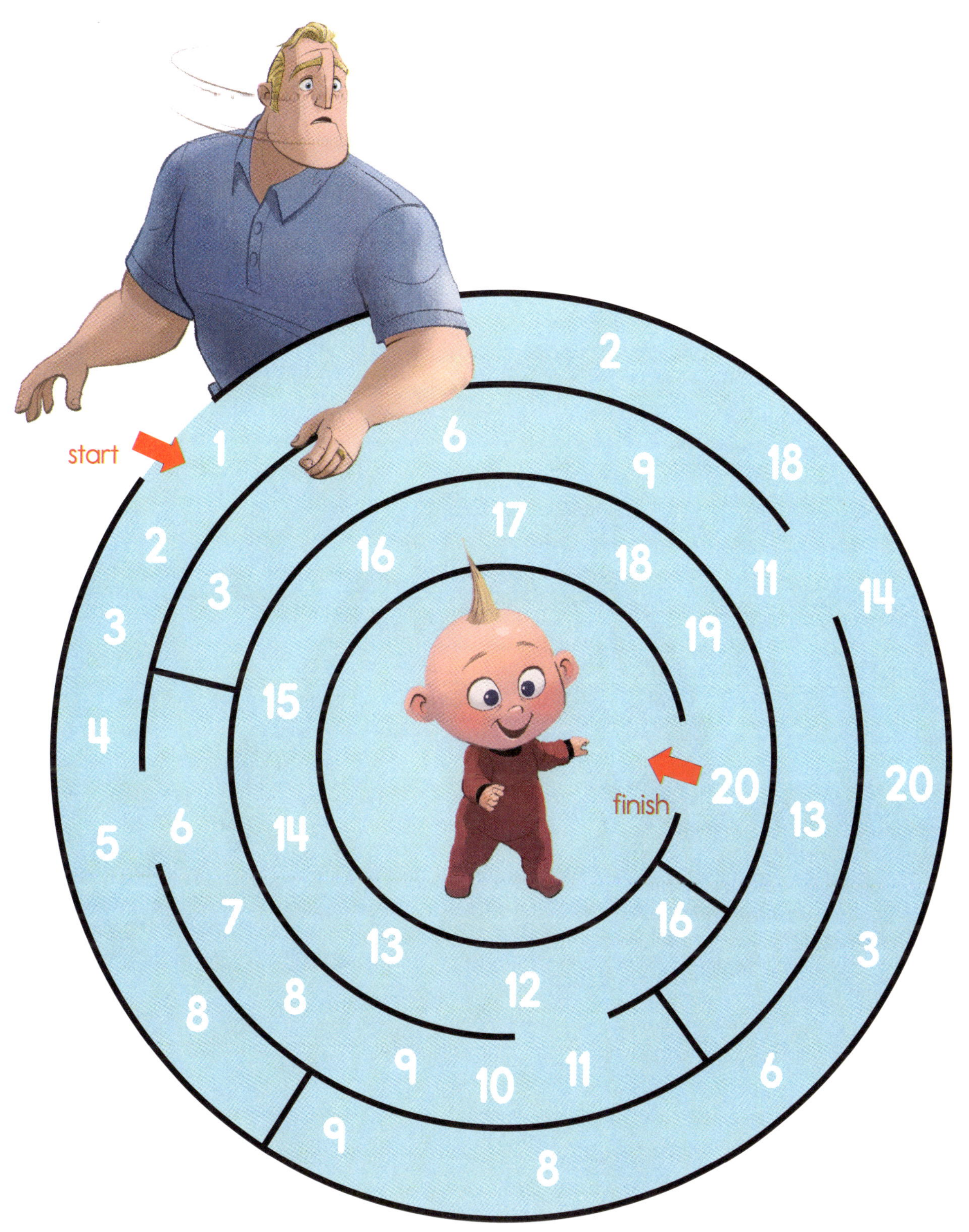

Bing-Bong is sad!

Count his candy tears.

Trace the numbers.

0 1 2 3 4 5

6 7 8 9 10

11 12 13 14 15

16 17 18 19 20

Learn Together

Count from 0 to 20 out loud with your child. Have a scavenger hunt to find 20 objects that are similar.

Connect the path from 1 to 20 to help Sulley catch Mike and Archie!

Congratulations

to

____

for completing this workbook!

Keep up the good work!

0 or zero means nothing.
Circle the objects that have nothing inside.

5

Circle the monster with 1 eye.

7

Joy and Sadness are collecting memory orbs.
Circle the group that has 2 memory orbs.

9

This monster has 2 heads!
Draw a monster with 3 heads.
Drawings will vary.
Monster should have 3 heads.

11

Circle 4 bottles for Jack-Jack.

13

Connect the dots from 0 to 5. Then, color.
0 start
1
2
3
4
5
finish

15

Help Elastigirl find Screenslaver!
Connect the path from 1 to 6.
start
finish

17

Draw more balls to make 7 in all.

19

Connect the numerals to the number words.
8
eight
8
eight

21

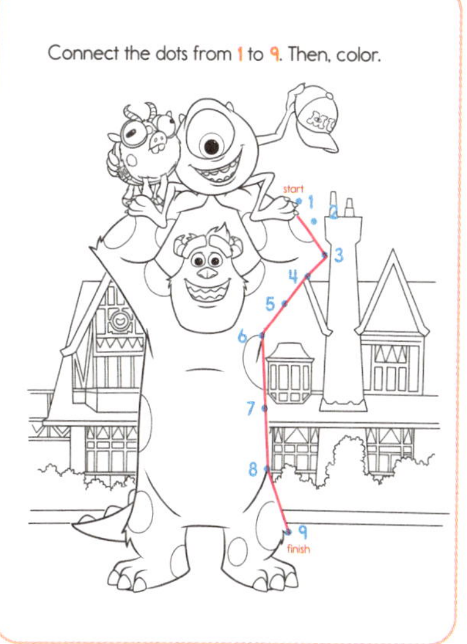
Connect the dots from 1 to 9. Then, color.
start
finish

23

Dash wants 10 strawberries for a snack.
Draw 10 strawberries on the plate.
Learn Together

25

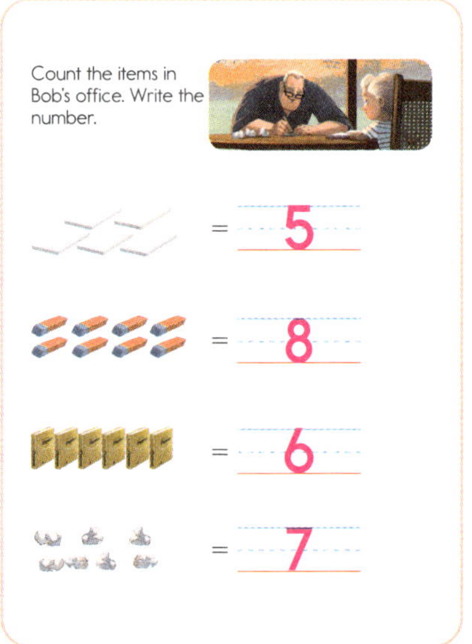
Count the items in Bob's office. Write the number.
= 5
= 8
= 6
= 7

26

Count the pens.
= 9
Count the books.
= 8
Count the trash cans.
= 4

27

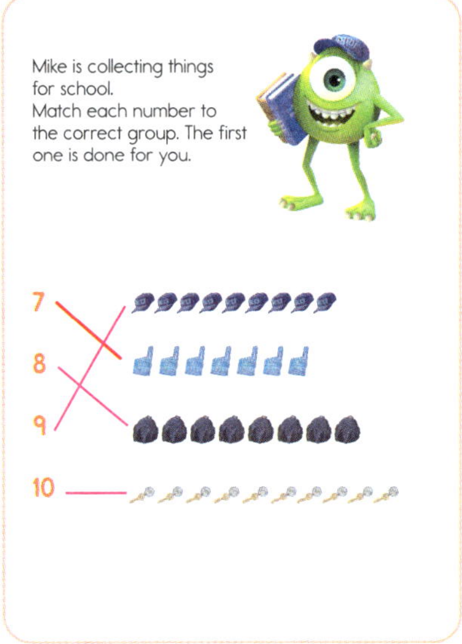
Mike is collecting things for school.
Match each number to the correct group. The first one is done for you.
7
8
9
10

28

How many books does Mike need? Match each number to the correct number of books. The first one is done for you.
7
8
9
10

29

Find the hidden 11s.

31

Mike needs 12 books for his classes. Draw more books to make 12.

33

Dash's locker is number 13. Circle it.

35

Circle 14 balloons.

37

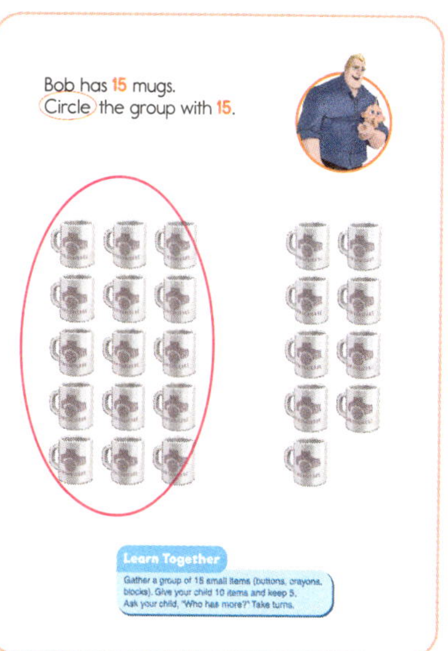
Bob has 15 mugs.
Circle the group with 15.

Learn Together
Gather a group of 15 small items (buttons, crayons, blocks). Give your child 10 items and keep 5. Ask your child, "Who has more?" Take turns.

39

Draw 16 memory orbs.

41

Draw a pizza with 17 toppings for Sulley.

43

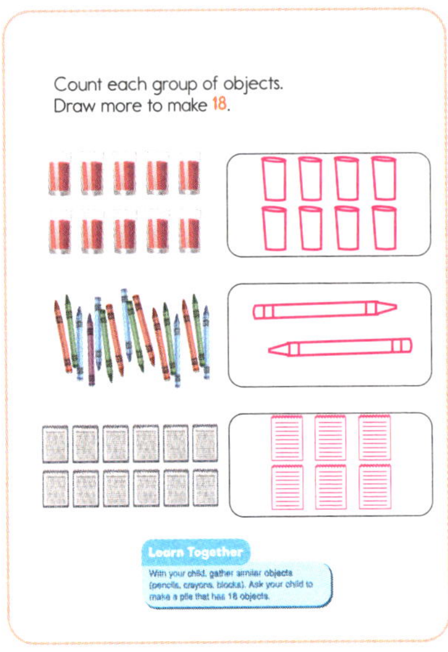
Count each group of objects.
Draw more to make 18.

Learn Together

With your child, gather similar objects (pencils, crayons, blocks). Ask your child to make a pile that has 18 objects.

45

Find the hidden 19s.

47

Find the hidden numbers 15 to 20.

49

Joy can count to 20.
Can you?

0 1 2 3 4 5
6 7 8 9 10
11 12 13 14 15
16 17 18 19 20

Print the missing numbers.

0 1 2 3 4

50

5 6 7 8 9 10
11 12 13 14 15
16 17 18 19 20
0 1 2 3 4
15 16 17 18 19
13 14 15 16 17

Learn Together

With your child, count objects around your home. Example: "How many books are on the shelf?" Encourage them to point to the objects and count out loud.

51

Connect the dots from 1 to 20. Then, color.

52

Help Bob find Jack-Jack. Connect the path from 1 to 20.
start
finish

53

Bing-Bong is sad!
Count his candy tears.
18

54

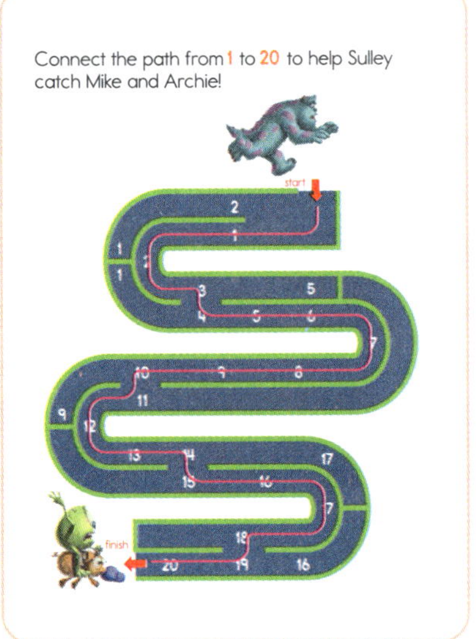
Connect the path from 1 to 20 to help Sulley catch Mike and Archie!
start
finish

56